Some Organized Chaos

(Poetry and Such)

Tumbleweed

authorHOUSE

AuthorHouse™
1663 Liberty Drive
Bloomington, IN 47403
www.authorhouse.com
Phone: 833-262-8899

Published by AuthorHouse 08/09/2023

ISBN: 979-8-8230-1249-2 (sc)
ISBN: 979-8-8230-1248-5 (e)

Print information available on the last page.

This book is printed on acid-free paper.

Dedicated to Norman and Marjorie Fechtig
And for my sons: Garth, Wolfgang, and Ozzy

The only time they ever seem to listen
Is when they read.
To most, my voice trails off, easily ignored,
But my pen does the deed,
And sadly it seems that I am only heard through my written word.
Maybe that's why my spirits dampen.

Contents

1

Crestfallen

Anger (I Am)

I am the storm that wakes you from your sleep.
I am the rain that leaks in and drips down.
I am the silence and the shadows that creep.
I am the lightning striking out all around.
I am the thunder lashing out as I weep.
I am your fear that's rising, changing smiles to frowns.
I am the nightmare that's keeping you awake.
I am all that is real in a world that's now fake.

Addiction

I am a slave to myself,
  To my basic desires,
    A primal lust.
I struggle to control my urges, myself.
  Still, my vices win;
    The strongest ones prevail.
The animal that lives within emerges,
  Comes alive savage with desire, lust,
    Knowing and getting what it wants.
My beast has been free for so long.
  I struggle to regain control.
    It is proud, selfish with its pleasures.

No Longer Sure of Who I Am

No longer sure of who I am,

I once thought I was quite the man.

But now it seems I'm not so sure.

I'm in need of help, seeking a cure,

Asking for advice or even a helping hand.

It's time for me to relearn what I once thought was right.

I'm tired of fighting; I want peace now in life.

I know the problems that I must fix,

But it'll take time, for change isn't quick.

And so, my son, I ask for your forgiveness

Because without you I am nothing, perhaps even less.

All the things I so wrongly knew

Led to all the bad habits that I used to do.

So I'll be your teacher and a much better dad

To make your life better, hoping it never gets this bad.

This Sinking Ship

I seek forgiveness
More so from myself than from anyone else.
I'm still haunted by my past actions,
The ones that consume me with regrets.
I cannot stop myself.
I turn my emotions inward.
My hate fills me with stress, rage,
The kind that feels beyond my control.

I am adrift in a sea of my own thoughts and worries,
With my fears being the storm into which I'm sailing.
Lost within myself with my vessel also sinking,
My ship taking on water too fast for me to bail out.
I, the captain of my own thoughts, now pay for my ignorance,
Fighting hard now to right all these wrongs
Before it becomes too late.
I struggle on alone, fearful of my fate.

The Man in the Mirror

Who is that there looking back at me?
How could that possibly be me?
Is that how I really look?
Is this how the rest of the world sees me?

This thing I see looking back at me—
Surely that cannot be me.
But he is all that I can see,
So logically, he has to be me.

But when did I become this?
How did I let this happen?
How did I lose myself this badly?

Am I really this monster that I see?
I feel him living within me,
So I guess maybe I am.

Sunset over a Mountain

I love you like a sunset over a mountain,
Every day changing,
Sometimes clouded in darkness
And others magnificently beautiful.
But much like a sunset,
That of day turning into night,
The light changing into darkness,
So are you,
And it is the darkness in you I fear,
For I can live in your light;
I can love you in it.
But your darkness frightens me
Like that of a violent storm.
Your lightning strikes out all around me,
And I fear it.
I can weather your storm no longer,
For as beautiful as it can be,
I can no longer stay to view it.
I must retreat to shelter, to safety.
I love you like the sunset over a mountain,
But it's time for me to watch the sunrise now
And to find the beauty within it—
The night giving birth to the day,
The light appearing out from the darkness—
And to feel safe within it,
Safe once more.

Poetic Therapy

Poetry in motion seems like slow motion.
Words come to mind flooded with emotion.
I try to write them all down; I try to keep up.
But the mind moves fast while the pen is slow.

I try to write to ease all my pains,
But my mind's grown dark like one huge stain.
So much emotional damage, a lot of baggage to claim.
Poetry seems to be the only thing keeping me sane.

I know more healthy coping methods are what I need,
But poetry seems to work the best for me indeed.
While trying to continuously rhyme is sometimes hard,
It's helped to ease the pains of life so far.

For it's always a daily struggle I seem to face,
Not just in the mind but also in this place.
And I am trying to change, to better myself,
Because happiness, I know, is the best kind of wealth.

I'm trying to stay strong both in body and mind,
But to keep myself going requires much effort and time.
Know that I will keep trying, though, and not just for me—
To be there for my son, for whatever he needs.

I Have Climbed Mountains

❖ ◆ ❖

I have climbed mountains and delved into caves.
I have traveled, seeing the world around me,
And yet you expect me to be your slave?
To chain me down like a dog, not allowed to roam free—
This is not who I am or who I will ever be.
I am meant to be wild; I am meant to be free.
And for you to remain in my life, you'll have to understand
You cannot control me, for I am my own man.

I have grown sick of your constant bullshit
And this pity-me party that you're throwing,
Trying to make me feel guilty when I am the one whom you bit.
I was the one who was wounded and hurt
With my injuries still showing,
For you left me all scarred up and broken,
And yet still you act like it was I who did you wrong.

For this, dear, you must be joking.
Go sing someone else your sad, sad song
Because I don't want to hear it anymore,
And it's wrong for you to be acting like this,
And you know this to be true.
It's because of you I'm still picking myself up from off the floor.

And I remain frightened of our recent past,
Having to dodge your fists and broken glass.
And it may be foolish of me to take you back,
Because I remember all your drunken attacks.
So like this mighty river, I must continue on
To regain my strength and feel proud and strong.

My Heart Aches

❖ ◆ ❖

My heart aches as the battle inside me rages on
With great sorrow and joy
And all the guilt that comes along with both.
It seems like a never-ending conflict resides within me,
For even when I feel happy, there is still so much misery.
But why then do I feel guilty for my happiness?
Is it from all my regrets and past actions?
Or the traumas I have yet to recover from?
I should be allowed to enjoy my happiness;
I must allow myself to do so,
Yet I don't know how, and so my heart aches.

My heart aches, afflicted by all my conflicting emotions,
All the struggles and the rage, all the passions and desires,
And all the guilt that follows them all.
How am I to conquer this inner turmoil of mine?
To once again freely be my happy old self,
To live without all the guilts and regrets of my past,
Must I forgive myself to again feel free?
This I do not know, and so my heart aches.

My heart aches, aches for me, longing to heal.
And I try, but try as I might,
I am still so lost, lost within myself,
My mind still filled with regret and sorrow
And my heart longing to feel intimacy

And be embraced once more.
But I fear I am afraid of love now,
That which has caused me so much pain and suffering,
Trapping me inside myself once again
To do battle with all my demons and miseries.
And that is why my heart aches.

My heart aches, now unable to trust in others, much less myself,
And it feels so wrong this judgment I pass,
For I want to live again, to love again.
I long for happiness and joy,
Yet I feel guilty for feeling any pleasure.
And I know it's wrong for me to feel this way,
For I'm not allowing myself to live completely.
All this holding myself back, not living to my life's fullest,
Too afraid of failures and setbacks,
Ones that may never come, and so my heart aches.

My heart aches, aches for me and my selfish ways,
For all my fears and longings.
I cling to all things negative,
Holding me a prisoner within myself.
And it's not right; this I do know,
For it only adds more to my inner conflict—
More fuel to a fire that's already raging out of control—
And I must change; I have to if I ever want to enjoy life again.
And so I struggle on, battling all my thoughts,
Fighting hard to quell this aching heart of mine
So I can feel the fires of passionate love once more,
Be overwhelmed by joyous happiness like never before,
And no longer have a heart that constantly aches.

To Be Held

❖ ❖ ❖

I wish to be held while I cry.

    Oh, how I long to feel the intimate touch of a lover's sweet embrace,

Holding me while I weep and sob,

Telling me not to worry and that everything will be OK.

    Oh, how I long to feel that gentle caress

Like that of a mother soothing her upset child.

I wish to release all the pain that I feel,

To lose all the misery that I have bottled up within me.

    Oh, how I long to be held.

    Oh, how I long to feel safe once more.

    Oh, to be held by a lover tenderly while I weep,

Held tightly and safe inside comforting arms,

Freeing me of my pains and sorrows,

Turning my tears of sadness into joy.

    Oh, how I long to trust again,

To allow myself to truly open up once more,

To allow myself to show weakness in front of another,

A sign of my ultimate and deepest love and trust,

My truest form of surrender,

The greatest of gifts I can give.

    Oh, how I long to be held by a lover,

To be back in a gentle, sweet embrace,

Allowing me to free myself as we become one,

Conjoined together in a tender and passionate embrace.

    Oh, how I wish to be held while I cry.

The King of Nothing

❖ ❖ ❖

I am the king of nothing,
For I have been dethroned.
With all my fortunes now all robbed
And my life no longer being my own,
I have been forced to start over
And made to do it all alone.

Everyone now wonders why I'm so unhappy.
Like is it really all that unclear?
I'm actually quite angry, pissed off at the world.
Losing my son was once my greatest fear,
But now so is the struggle of raising him alone.
Lost I am without you near.

I am the king of nothing,
For it has all been taken from me,
And I am no longer free to do what I like,
A prisoner in a false world of recovery.
Will this nightmare ever end?
Or am I trapped in this hell called "sobriety"?

There are all these eyes on me.
It feels like my every move is watched.
How did it all come down to this?

A momentary lapse in judgment has caused all my hope to be lost,
And I know that I did wrong; I know that I fucked up.
But of these sins, they will not let me wash.

I am the king of nothing.

Every Time I Stumble and Fall

Every time I stumble and fall,

You are there, making the hole deeper,

Making my falls greater.

I am tired of these nasty spills.

I am tired of nursing my wounds.

I want my scars to fade away,

But you are a constant reminder

Of all the pain you have caused me.

The emotional wounds cut just as deeply as the physical ones,

And I wear the scars as proof.

I am a survivor,

But now I just want to relax.

And I don't think that that's too much to ask.

Paranoia

I feel like the world is conspiring against me,
Like it wants me to live in a state of constant misery,
For my happiness doesn't matter to those in control.
I'm just a puppet for their amusement, putting on a show,
And to be honest, I am fed up with it all.
I am tired of this outside interference.
I want to be able to live my life without putting on a false appearance.
I want to be who I truly am at all times
And not have to hide away as if being me is a crime.
But will all this ever end?
Or will it all just begin again,
One great endless cycle of misery,
Where the only one I can trust is me?

The Violence of Man

The violence of man is on the rise
As we kill the world around us
While also killing each other,
Letting innocent children die, murdered.
It's become hard now to determine who to trust,
Causing us all to have to suffer more.

There is a sickness among men,
One that has always been there.
Now festered and worse,
There's violence taking place in all lands.
The toll of this can be seen everywhere:
Man's greed and bloodthirst.

Tired

I'm tired,
Saddened by the fact
      That I have grown used to sleeping alone,
My bed empty, open beside me
With your presence no longer present.
      Out of sight has become out of mind.

I'm tired,
But I'm still able to sleep,
      Hoping that you can too.
We had so much together,
Now all just memories.
      The joyous ones are good; I'm learning from the bad.

I'm tired.
I just put our son to bed,
      And now I'm unsure what to do.
But I'm tired.
I might just go to bed,
      Just go in there and lie down.

Sitting with Myself
(Late-Night Thoughts)

❖ ❖ ❖

I sit here still and in silence,
Yet my mind stays loud with chaos,
With so many thoughts, possibilities.
But I just sit here, doing nothing,
So much wasted potential.
It's disgraceful, and I hate myself for it,
But I make no effort to try or change.
I sit content in my boredom,
Content in my selfish ways.

I sit here alone and in silence.
I hear the world going on around me.
It is carrying on fine without me
As I simply just sit, listening to it.
I could go back, join the world,
Rejoin society if I choose.
I could open this door and step out into the night,
Yet I remain still, seated, listening,
Living only half a life, it seems.
Why do I choose this for myself?
I want to be happy too.

I've been told I deserve it, but do I?
Am I worthy of living a happy life?
All I have to do is choose it,
Yet I am content,
So I make no new efforts.
Why complicate what's simple?
Why try if I don't have to?

Am I Lazy?

Am I lazy? Content in my laziness?
I want to do what's best for me,
But I don't know what that even is.
Maybe I am unable to change,
Or maybe I am just still yet unwilling,
Afraid of change, so I avoid it.
But change will always find me
And force me to adapt,
Whether I want to or not,
Whether I'm ready to or not.
I will always have to face it,
So why do I not just embrace it?
Surely it would make my life so much easier.
Why is my anxiety so reluctant to change?
So overpowering that I'd rather suffer hardship?
What happened that made me this way?
What shaped my core beliefs to this
And set my life down this darkened path?
How do I recover? Or can I?
Am I capable of changing?
I surely do hope so.

Callow

❖ ❖ ❖

Left callow from the alcohol
And hollowed out by depression,
A man-child of now almost thirty,
I am still unable to function properly,
For if I'm left to my own devices,
I choose alcohol, my favorite of vices.
And all the poor choices that follow
Are my fault, I know, for I choose to be this shallow.
My darkness is haunting
And my challenges now daunting,
For my biggest fears have all come to life,
And overcoming them all is a bitter strife.
Yet the problem that remains
Is that I'm still left callow and filled with pain,
A hollow void afraid of making change.

Hurt

❖ ◆ ❖

1

I was hurt,

Wounded on the outside, physically

Traumatized inside, both mentally and emotionally.

I was hurt and needed to heal.

I was hurt, and I became lost,

Lost in my process of healing,

Struggling to find my way forward

Or to find my way back,

To be able to live again,

And to feel whole,

To be worthy of love once more.

I was hurt and in pain.

I was consumed by numbness,

Empty and alone.

I was hurt

And unsure of how to continue, how to proceed,

For my pain was immense

Because it was you who had hurt me.

2

I was hurt,

And in my pain, I became foolish, reckless,

Overwhelmed by simply living life.

Because I was hurt, I was lost. I was alone,

And I struggled to find my way.

All the alcohol I consumed was of no help,

But I was hurt, and so I drank,

And my choices became unwise.

I was foolish and selfish in my nature.

I was lost and looking to be found in all the wrong directions

Because I was hurt,

And I didn't want to feel anymore.

And in my pain and hurt,

I made my biggest mistakes.

Drunk and not thinking clearly,

I put my life in danger,

But more importantly,

I put his little life in danger.

I was hurt, but this hurts me more.

3

I was hurt, and I self-destructed.

Lost within myself, I crawled inside a bottle.

I was hurt and now totally alone,

My son no longer with me, removed from my care,

Residing now in another's home.

I was hurt, and that pain was great;

And I wanted to numb it, to end it,

To heal my aching heart,

To stop all my negative thoughts.

For now, I was lost, worse than ever before,

And so fearful of my coming future.

I was hurt, but I did it to myself.

Unsure of how to heal,

I finally had to ask for help,

For I was only getting worse,

For I was hurt and on my own,

Lost, broken, and without a home.

4

I was hurt, but now I'm healing,
For I have found my way back.
Now I'm walking on the right path,
But I was hurt, and my pain was great.
I let my life spiral down, out of control.
Things have gotten better now.
Many lessons I have learned,
And only a few bridges did I burn.
I was hurt, and I was lost.
I wanted to quit many times.
I wanted to give up, give in, let the liquor win.
But I never gave up, even though I hurt.
I fought through all my pain
So I could reclaim my life
And be reunited with my son again.
I was hurt, but I learned to overcome.
I was hurt, but I learned how to heal.

The Quick-Tempered Trouble

My emotions sometimes get the best of me,
> For I am not a patient man.

But I do try so hard to be.
> I am quick to anger and quick to sin.

And every time I lose my temper,
> I have to start over again.

I want to be better; I'm trying my hardest,
> But my progress remains slow.

But I am maintaining my course;
> I'm not giving in to the flow.

Life for me has been so difficult.
> No one taught me how to live.

I had to learn everything on my own,
> Never learning how to forgive.

Now all these grudges I hold;
> They're eating me alive.

I'm fighting a daily battle,
> Simply to live, longing to thrive.

The Folly of Man

❖ ❖ ❖

The screen I stare at hurts my head,
>Yet I continue to stare.
I should be folding the laundry on my bed,
>But I just don't really care.
I'm addicted to my phone,
>Just like so many others,
Slaves to the screens we welcome in our homes.
>What once was entertainment now smothers.
Is there any hope left for mankind?
>Not on this path we currently walk,
For we have all become so blind
>And so foolish when we talk,
Arrogant and selfish in our ways.
>But to live in this world, we must change,
Or our kids will see the end of days,
>And we will be the ones to blame.

Talking to a Wall

The madness I feel
>All trapped within me.

A shadow-handed deal.

>How could it possibly be?

Am I starting to come out on top?

Or will this run of good luck come to a stop?

I struggle so hard, trying to give a fuck.

>I'm honestly quite selfish, you see,

But you don't care if the truth comes out.

No matter what, you scream and shout.

You don't care about me, only you.

So, is this love one that's really true?

Who Am I?

❖ ❖❖ ❖

A question I have always asked,
     And at one time an answer I thought I knew,
But that is now all just a fleeting memory,
     Gone like all the days of yesterday.

I know not who I am,
     For I am just myself.
Is there any more to me than that?
     That's another question I have always asked.

The Realization

❖ ❖ ❖

I am a man filled with lust,

      Burning up with passions and desires,

But I am also a man filled with fear,

      Overflowing with anxiety and dread.

I want to feel happy

      And be satisfied,

But I no longer know what I am doing.

      It feels like my life has become a lie.

Every day is the same.

      I wake up, and there is no change.

I feel so old now,

      And my body is shutting down.

How did all of this happen?

      I never stood a chance.

When I Close My Eyes

❖ ◈ ❖

I see the us we were when I close my eyes,
But open, I see the us we have become.
I see how different we have become, how changed.

It seems like life was more rough on us than good,
But that could also be from all the poor choices we made.
By having no one there to guide us, we forged our own path.
It was their celebrating the mediocrity that cast us out; we became lost.
Now hated by those once close, once held dear,
Betrayed by them as they dragged us down,
Encouraging our bad behaviors to make themselves feel better.
They helped us reach our traumatic downfall.

Now forced to be apart, we recovered alone.

So here I stand, a changed man.
Why then do I still feel the same inside as I always have?
I feel my life is just a cycle of loops on repeat,
And I have not yet figured out how to break their cycle.
I am a prisoner of anxiety, trapped within my mind.
It's like a cold, damp, wet stone cell;
And there I sit within, meditating on my failure.
I bring myself down low and struggle to rise back up,
For it is hard for me to love myself,
And I fear that has darkened me, perhaps even down to my soul.

I don't like seeing me when I close my eyes.

The Rat King

The Rat King has made his demands,
But his words will not be heeded,
For no one fears the Rat King anymore.
His fame and glory have long since retreated.
And though the rats he still commands,
He reigns over the shadows; nothing more.

Drowning in Misery from Deep Within

Drowning in misery from deep within,
I seem filled with a darkness that has no end,
Leaving me to wish I could be myself again.
My happiness is fleeting, leaving only pain.
My sadness is growing, fueled by my shame.
I'm wondering now if I'll ever again be the same.

My Thoughts Are Clouded

❖ ❖ ❖

My thoughts are clouded, and my mind is now racing.

I seem unable to focus on the small tasks I'm undertaking

How can this be? Your face keeps drifting up, visualizing you from memory,

Yet now you are a stranger to me, one I cannot recognize,

For it was your previous actions that changed both our lives,

Plunging us both alone into new chaos so different from the past.

And now from my own actions I am lost, desperately seeking the right path,

For I know you are not entirely to blame. I am the cause of most of my shame,

But I can see a light through the darkness,

The stars shining through the trees.

So, I will just catch my breath and try to carry on with ease.

Recovery

❖ ❖ ❖

I have matured so much
And all within such a short time.
It once felt like it'd take forever,
Back when I was lost, out of touch,
But I overcame, I conquered,
Fighting for what is mine,
Making things all slowly get better.
And I don't care about the rumors you've heard,
For I am now a much better person
Than I ever was before
Because I did it all for my son,
For I know he needs me more.

Time to Rejoice

I feel like it is time to celebrate,
>   For this battle has been hard won,
Yet I fear starting too prematurely,
>   For the fight is not all the way done.

And one success does not make me the victor.
>   There are still several things left to do,
For if I were to celebrate too early,
>   This whole, long process I might again have to go through.

I have worked far too hard,
>   And I will not be starting again all over,
But I want to be able to reward myself
>   One simple treat, nothing too grandeur.

Just to relax in the evenings,
>   Not roister the night away,
For I have learned from all those mistakes,
>   And that's no longer how I want to spend my day.

2

Fatherhood

High Chair Thoughts

Cleaning up after you got to bed,
Putting away all the toys and books,
    And picking up all the scattered food bits,
Seeing what all you ate or didn't,
What all you dropped or tried to hide away.
Your high chair holds your diary of the day.
It fills me in on how you're feeling.
Breakfast, lunch, and dinner are all recorded there,
Showing me all that you liked and what you didn't.
I reminisce over the day we had
    And how we spent it together.
How did you feel? Did you have fun?
    Did I teach you any valuable life lessons?
Cleaning up before I head to bed
So tomorrow can begin anew
To wake up and have a fresh start.

Ode to My Son

❖ ❖ ❖

Crazy bed head, early morning riser,
The first to wake up and the first to go to bed,
My little boy, my pride and joy.
With that crazy blond hair, wild upon your head,
You make my whole world brighter.

Warrior of Chaos

It seems all I do is clean
So he can make a mess anew,
Like scattering all his blocks
Or pulling down all his books,
Rearranging what all I had just arranged
Faster than the blink of an eye,
My little warrior of chaos.

A Perfect Morning

An early morning,
A fresh start, a new day.
Life feels good today.
There's happiness in the air.

Breakfast is being made.
There's coffee brewing in the pot.
I just smoked a bowl in my room
On this cool December morning.

My son playing with all his toys
Or watching Mama cook or me type.
He's so fascinated by my typewriter.
I can't wait to teach him on it someday.

What will we do with the rest of this day?
The weather reports that it will warm up some,
So I think a walk sounds like a splendid idea
For us to get out and enjoy some fresh air.

Winter Preparations

The cold chill of the approaching winter fills the air.

I can feel it in the numbing of my hands

As I see snow starting to appear on the mountains.

It is still October, but fall now seems to have ended.

Soon these golden and orange leaves will be covered in white,

And I do not feel prepared for it.

But there is also nothing I can do to stop it either,

For the weather is something beyond what I can control,

But I like winter. I like the snow and the cold,

To layer up with coats and hats,

To tramp through the snow with my boots on.

I do not know how my son will feel about winter, though.

He is now one and just beginning to walk.

It will be exciting to see him play in the snow,

To witness his reactions and expressions,

For he is quite the little character,

To see him in my old snowsuit,

Kept safe by Grandma all this time.

Teaching him how to stay warm

And the importance of things he does not quite yet understand.

I am his father, and he is my son,

But we are both teachers and students,

Learning from each other the importance of life and family.

He is my world, and I will take care of him

The best that I can.

Early Morning, and I Am the First to Awake

❖ ❖❖ ❖

Early morning, and I am the first to awake.

As the sun shines in warm through the windows,

I sit back, trying to relax,

Trying to find my peace,

While my early summer allergies take their toll.

I'm just trying to breathe

Yet constantly having to blow my nose to do so,

But the endless snot has got my sinuses blocked.

I know it'll be a good day.

It'd just be better if I could breathe right.

Nana's Visit

My son has been sleeping for an hour by now,
Yet I still sit here, wide awake, puffing on
My pipe and reminiscing on how,
On how this visit with Grandma has gone.
She's leaving for home in the morning,
Flying back to the land of Missouri,
And I know her grandson she'll miss adoring,
Simply spoiling him rotten so surely.

Bedtime Routines

The child refuses to go to sleep.
He's fighting it hard,
      Causing his mother to start to weep.
The child refuses to rest his head.
He's tossing and turning about
      Back and forth across his bed.

I Sit Watching My Son Play

❖ ❖ ❖

I sit watching my son play,
Thinking of the man he'll be one day,
Of all the lessons I'll have to teach,
Getting up to move things out of his reach,
Having to teach him that life isn't fair.

I think back to how my father raised me
And about the kind of father I want to be,
Of all the choices I will have to make,
Knowing that some of them will be a mistake,
Hoping he knows that I'll always care.

The View Outside

Looking out the window, I see
A lady out painting her house,
Her ass in short shorts, jean cutoffs.
I watch as she climbs up and down the ladder.
The bacon I'm cooking burns.
"I hope you like it extra crispy."
I don't because it hurts my teeth.

From dark gray to white,
Just the first layer of primer.
What color is next to come?
I am excited to see,
Not about the painting but about the view.
The day is still cool, yet I notice
Sweat starting to glisten in the early-morning sun.
Quite the distraction for me.

My son plays with toys, watching his movie,
But I'm looking out the window,
Munching on some crunchy bacon
And witnessing a true sight of beauty.
Not to be creepy and not to be rude,
But that booty makes for one spectacular view,
And there's not a whole lot else going on for me to do.

My Evening Meditations

❖ ❖ ❖

My evening meditations,
A time for me to gather my thoughts,
To reflect on what I've done today
And on what still needs to be done tomorrow.
As I try to prepare for bed,
This is my time to relax.
Sitting in silence, I find peace.
Quieting my mind, I focus on my breath.
This is my evening meditation,
And this day is nearing its end,
Readying myself for tomorrow
To face a new day with calmful Zen
By bringing forth the wisdom I've learned
Of today and all the yesterdays
So that all things come into balance.
I practice my evening meditations.

Nap Time's Ending

My son is sleeping soundly in his room.
As his nap extends further into the night,
"Should I wake him?" I ask myself.

I enjoy the quiet peace I have
But I know I should wake him soon
So that he'll sleep again when bedtime comes.

I'll give him just a little more time,
For maybe if by chance he stays up late,
He might sleep in longer tomorrow morning.

A longshot dream, not a hope just a thought,
But there …
I think I hear him.

An Observation

❖ ❖ ❖

I sit watching my son play,

    Thinking of the man he'll be one day,

Of all the lessons there are to teach,

    All the things I must keep out of reach,

Having to show him that life isn't fair.

I think back to how my father raised me

    And what all I'm going to do differently,

Of all the choices that I will have to make

    And being able to forgive myself for my mistakes,

Hoping he knows that I'll always be there.

Dinnertime

❖ ◆ ❖

Trying to stand up in his high chair,
Making me nervous of a coming fall,
He's refusing to eat his dinner.
Too fascinated by my clicking typewriter,
He's watching me while I work away,
Wanting, longing to participate
Or for me to release him down, to play.
But he must eat his dinner first.

Evening Yoga

Evening yoga
    After my son goes to bed.
Now it's my quiet time.   Meditation,
My time to reflect on my day,
A time to wind down before bed.
A chance to calm my mind, soul, and body.
My special time,   just a bit of personal time.
A time for me,
    My time.
And I hold it sacred,
    My evening yoga.

He Didn't Take a Nap Today

He didn't take a nap today.
We were on the go all afternoon,
But he did sleep in late this morning
And for the first time in a long time too.

A Fatherhood Fragment

❖ ❖ ❖

Fatherhood has indeed straightened me out quite a bit,

For now that I'm sober, my clothes are getting snug to the fit,

And I'm doing all that I can to live my best life right,

Finally starting to see all my dreams come to light.

For now, I finally feel less lost,

But on that journey, I paid a heavy cost.

But now it is time for me to live again.

Hands in Pockets

I see you have learned how your pockets work, my son,
Standing there, laughing at your movie playing,
Your face glowing with joy.
A mental image for me to cherish forever
Just to see you standing there,

      Your hands in your pockets,
      Radiating total bliss.
      It brings me so much joy,
      For I can close my eyes
      And see you in such perfect detail.

It fills me with so much warmth,
For you are growing up so fast
And learning so much so quick.

      I love to see you smile,
      For it always brings me joy,
      And that helps bring me peace.

Early Bird

The sun has risen,
And the day loon since has started,
But I am just now slowly rising,
Yet the rest of my family still sleeps.

It is a quiet and lonely morning
As I sit here alone,
Pondering how to spend my time,
For everyone will wake soon no matter what.

So how should I spend this moment in time?
Poetry and books? Yoga and meditation?
I simply close my eyes and breathe
When I hear my son stir in his room.

Adjustment Period

❖ ❖ ❖

Apartment living is not for me.
Sharing walls with other people
    Is not a fun or pleasant time.
I miss my mountain
    And the life she provides.

For I do not enjoy the sound of others' laughter.
I always feel it is at my expense,
That I am the butt of all their jokes.
Great waves of paranoia rush over me.
My anxiety and tensions rise,
    And it is not a fun or pleasant time.
Oh, how I miss my mountain
    And the life she provides.

City life is no life for me.
There're too many people everywhere we go.
None of them really know what they're doing,
All just mindless sheep following a greedy wolf,
One who is no longer disguised as a shepherd even,
Pitting us all against our own neighbors,
Laughing as we struggle on.
    But for us, it's not a fun or pleasant time,
And oh, how I miss my mountain
    And the life she provides.

The Neighbor

"Why do you think she has so many kids?"
To her a baby is an accessory,
A plaything to show off as an extension of herself,
Satisfying her needs for attention.

But toddlers are a pain in the ass,
And once they can be independent, on their own,
The cycle just sadly repeats.
All the kids take care of each other,
The bigger ones raising the younger,
Unsure of what they're doing themselves.
They have no one there to guide them,
For their mother is too self-absorbed,
Lost within her selfish vanities and lust.

It's honestly quite very sad,
And I do feel bad for those children.

A Small Piece of Wisdom

I feel that life is fake,
And I am so tired of love and heartache.
I just want to fade out ... away.
But I love my son, and so I stay.

He is my world, and I do my honest best,
Juggling him and all of life's tests.
See, his mother makes things extra hard,
Always looking for a way to play her card.

She drives me absolutely crazy.
Now look. I'm fat, unemployed, and lazy.
I just want to give up and get drunk,
But I need to be a father, not a dumbass punk.

But what does it mean to be a great dad?
Is it handling our emotions, especially those which are sad?
By learning how to simply process and how to heal,
One can truly teach one a great deal.

A Poem for Grandpa

Last night you died.
They say you went peacefully and
That helps me to feel a little better.

I miss you greatly,
But I wish I could have seen you
At least one last time.

I wanted you to meet my son,
Who'd be your great-grandson.
I know you would've loved him.

But I still feel bad
That you two never got to meet.
If only the distance between us wasn't so great.

I wish I could be there,
There to attend your funeral,
Yet we live so far apart.

I miss you,
And I love you,
And I always will.

3
Journeying

What Journey Awaits Me? (Today)

❖ ◆ ❖

Paddling this kayak down the rivers of my mind,
And it has me now lost within a jungle,
A jungle of my thoughts.

Parts of these rivers I know quite well,
While some of the others seem untouched,
And I am wearisome of those unknown waters.

I am afraid of the newness, change,
But that is what I'm exploring today,
Adventuring into the unknown I hold within.

Channeling the Moon Doggie

❖ ◆ ❖

"I write poetry, you little bitch."

1

A little booze, a little weed, a little poontang,
All the fun little goodies that make life worth living,
'Cause I'm here for a good time, not a long time,
And I'm just trying to make the most of it
And live it at my best while I can,
Because the worlds become a very scary place to be.
So much hate, violence, and greed live within my fellow man.
We've become ignorant, foolish, and proud, caring only for ourselves.
A society primed and headed toward collapse.
Am I helping to make things better? Are you?

2

I smoked two joints, and I threw up,
Puked right into my trash can,
So at least there's no mess to clean,
And I just filled up my cup.
I'm back to being a drinking man,
Though I fear the rum, how it makes me mean.
But I'm pacing myself, and I'm keeping my cool
'Cause I don't want to wind up again being the fool.

3

Orange juice poured into a forty,
Helping me to kick back and relax
After a long and shitty day.
I just want to smoke some weed, fuck you down dirty.
Things to help get my mind back on track,
Sculpting my new self up from out of clay
Because I have become my own god
While the one you worship remains a fraud.

4

Is it all just some twisted practice?
A cruel, harsh warm-up
Before the real beatdown takes place?
Not surprising; the world's so full of malice,
Knocking you down further when you already have no luck
And no trust with people lying straight to your face.
Everyone just simply wants to be famous.
People will do anything; they've become completely shameless.

5

A strong mixture of liquor and weed
Does, in fact, do the deed,
But it isn't long lasting. Sad but true.
I must keep going to avoid those hangover blues.
And that's a strong recipe for disaster
Because the liquor will quickly become my master,
But it's so hard to drink responsibly
When life just remains so constantly shitty.
Oh, but it helps me to feel oh so good.

6

Living with a liquor store in the neighborhood,
Only being just a block or two away.
It's a quick, little walk made once or twice a day.
And some do say my drinking is a problem,
But it's not my problem, only theirs.
I just give it all no worries.
I'm just trying to enjoy my story.
I want to live my life happily,
And fuck you for wanting me to feel so crappy.

Here I Am

And so, here I stand,
Storybook in hand,
Wanting to be my best,
Dreaming of a better life,
Waiting for something
>That will not happen
>If I do not act.
>And now is the time for action.

And so, here I sit
While a battle rages within,
Fighting the urges to stare into my phone,
To disappear simply into the void,
Lost, enslaved by a screen,
>Fighting for my freedom.
>But addiction is so cruel,
>And I must conquer mine.

And so, here I lie,
Wrestling myself to sleep,
Longing to drift off to dreams,
Hoping for a restful slumber,
And fantasizing of relaxing.
>But none of it helps,
>For I am not tired,
>For I have done nothing today.

And so, here I am,
Staying up late, alone,
Thinking and overthinking,
My nightly meditations,
My evening philosophies.

      I am slowly changing.
      I'm working on being better.
      Maybe then I can help you be better too.

Flashback

In a meditative state, it appeared to me,
The forest I wandered in during my teenage youth.
It was all so real and familiar,
Like I was there once again.
I felt waves of emotion rush over me.
"Oh ... What is this?" I cried.
Loneliness. It was loneliness.
In these woods, I wandered alone,
Longing for adventure,
Searching for some kind of magic,
Hoping to finally find someone to call a friend.

These old feelings of loneliness
Swept over me with great intensity,
And I felt as if I had figured it out.
What? I don't know, but the puzzle pieces all clicked in,
Bringing me a small moment of peace.

Is there a part of my soul still trapped there,
Alone in the woods, seeking a friend,
Still longing for his great adventure?

Would a journey back bring me any answers?

Alien Day

❖ ❖ ❖

The half-moon still visible, vivid, and bright,
Present high up in the clear morning sky,
Standing out, proud, defiant, and alone,
As if challenging the sun for space.

The world seems so alien today.
Our morning walk feels strange, almost unnatural,
And as I see the planes flying above us overhead,
I know that today will be different, special.

I can sense the magic as we walk,
Even though it's the same route as every day.
Today it just feels so different and new,
As if it's the first time we have ever walked it.

I can see the beauty all around us,
And I am in love with this new alien world,
For my eyes have now been opened,
And I am now lost within the world around me.

What is so special about this day? This walk?
Is it that the moon is still gracing us with her presence?
A truly beautiful and yet so simple of a sight to behold
Has now changed my entire perception of the world.

For all these sights around me, I have seen them all before,
Yet today they are so new and wondrous through my new eyes.
I stumble now as I walk through the new world,
Amazed at the clarity and beauty of all things around me.

I feel happiness in the sunshine,
And as the cool morning wind blows,
I can sense summer ready to change to fall.
Will this new alien world change along with it?

The half-moon, still high up in the sky,
Has altered my reality and my entire life,
For it's remarkable all the power that she holds,
Her ability to control the whole world around us.

A sight of true beauty, one I am lucky to see
As she stands defiant in the blue morning sky.
I am thankful that she allowed me to witness her,
Incredibly grateful for her presence and perfection.

Why Did I Buy Three Big Red Bulls?

❖ ❖ ❖

Too much caffeine, two tall Red Bulls.

My heart is pounding, my hands are shaking.

My thoughts are racing as my mind runs wild.

I try to breathe, to regain control,

But I can't; I lack the focus required.

I just have to maintain, to power through.

The effects will fade away,

And things will soon normalize,

But I know that I'll do it again

Because I always seem to,

Yet maybe one day I'll learn.

Maybe one day I'll stop

If I master myself, my self-control,

But that all takes time,

And time requires energy,

For it's a game playing with fire.

Too much caffeine, those two Red Bulls,

Not to mention the one still left in the fridge.

The Water Ride

I fell out of the canoe.
It flipped over and dumped me out,
Sending me floating down the river.
I was cast out,
Now splashing about in the white water,
Fighting to keep my head up,
Fighting for my breath
As I tumble down the rapids,
Slamming up against the rocks.
I am pushed and pulled along,
Gripped by fear and panic,
Still recovering from the shock.
I struggle to stay afloat,
Hoping that the river calms ahead
And that I can hang on until then,
My whole body now aching and cold.
Flailing out, I grasp a branch.
A fallen tree comes to my salvation.
I struggle to pull myself up,
Hoping the limb doesn't snap off,
Dumping me back into the water.

Doc

Swindled by a man with a false name
And a fake idea to go with a false persona,
Nothing about him was ever real,
Except for the darkness hidden inside,
A darkness he tried so hard to hide.
And I fell for the act at first
Like so many others before me, now after me.
He played me out like a game,
Used me for all that he could,
Robbing me of all my hard work
With his laziness and lies.
And finally, when I had had enough,
It was my leaving that angered him,
For he was now no longer in control.
I had taken it back for me,
Having to correct all his lies with the truth,
All because I was swindled by a man,
Swindled by a man with a false name.

The Pattern

The pattern simply repeats.
The pattern always repeats.
Study the histories.
Study your life.
Just look around you.
The pattern repeats itself.
The pattern simply repeats.
The pattern always repeats.
Study the histories.
      You'll find plenty.
Study your life.
      Look back and reflect.
Just look around you.
      What all do you see?
The pattern repeats itself.
The pattern simply repeats.
The pattern always repeats.

Opening the Channel

❖ ❖❖ ❖

I am in a hammock in the woods,
Set up between two trees,
Two pines.

My camp is near a river.
I can see the water, hear it too.
There's a nice breeze blowing.

My hammock sways in the breeze,
And I am totally relaxed, at peace.
I am present.

There is a canoe on the bank by the river.
I go and climb into it,
And I begin to paddle.

The water is so beautiful,
Like the rest of the world around it.
I focus on paddling.

I feel myself in a rhythm,
One I enjoy greatly,
The dance of the canoe.

The land opens,
Opens to reveal a beautiful valley.
I paddle onward.

An Incident of Violence

There's a young man sitting on the floor.
He has his back against the wall,
And he's crying as he rocks,
Going forward and back, hugging his knees.

His head is badly bleeding
While his hands smear blood and tears everywhere.
He is confused, in shock,
Lost as if frozen in time.

All around him, he sees her yelling.
He sees her fists flying toward him, at him,
Yet he no longer feels them connecting.
He's barely conscious now.

Suddenly, there's a loud bang.
A bright light appears
Along with black, shadowy figures.
The young man's face hits the ground, unconscious.

A Moment in Time

Standing there in the darkness of my bedroom doorway,
I see a shadow, a tear in space,
Darkness calling me in.

I enter into a moment.
Turning on the lights,
      I sit and pick up my son's toy rattle.
The sound lures him in.

He takes the rattle from me,
And as he begins to play on his own,
I stare, lost, looking at his wild hair.
      Zen.

When I rise, emerging back into presence,
I emerge back into action, back into focus.
I emerge once again, ready for the task at hand.

People Watching

❖ ❖ ❖

There's a man sitting in his car
Alone at the far side of the parking lot.
His engine is off, has been for a while.
He seems very anxious like he's waiting on something.

What could he be waiting for? I wonder.
I have spent lots of time in parking lots.
I have been where he is. Did I look like that? Like him?
At my worst, I may have been lower.

There's a man sitting in his car.
His face is rough from a long life led,
Yet he does not look too terribly old.
But as experienced as he may be, he now looks lost within.

What all has been done? I wonder.
I have been lost and searching too
And found still unsure of which step to take first,
There at the finding of wisdom, peace, and patience.

There's a man sitting in his car.
He's digging around in his mess,
A cluttered collection of his life,
All his possessions within easy arm's reach.

There's a man sitting in his car,
Just trying to live his own life.
We make eye contact as he notices me staring.
I turn away and go back to my business.

Snow Tires and Road Closures

❖ ❖ ❖

I must keep my mind in a positive frame
And stop this winter depression from staking its claim,
From dragging me down, making me go insane.
I am stressed out over all the snow,
That which is far out of my control.
Imprisoned by this winter weather,
Depression not helping to make things any better,
I'm trapped inside, lonely and isolated,
My problems and anxieties now consolidated.
And by checking the weather every few minutes,
My worries are starting to push their limits.
My mind enters into a darker place
As I try to conceal the worry from my face.
But I am troubled, and I am scared,
And with winter here, I just want to be prepared.

A Letter to the Snow

❖ ◆ ❖

My dearest winter,

Your arrival seems so soon.

It seems I barely had a summer,

For you had only just left,

And now you're already back again.

It feels so sudden though we foresaw you coming.

Now I regret not enjoying the warmth of summer more.

Your cold, wet beauty of this December mush only lasts so long.

      Sincerely, C.

A Trip in the Woods

❖ ❖ ❖

"The keys are lost," I say
      After one last frantic search,
"Unless one of you has them."
No one else does.
"Oh shit" and worse,
      Both said and thought.
"What are we going to do?" she asks.
"Retrace our steps and hope for the best," I answer.
And by the look on her face, she is not happy with me,
      Not happy with me at all.
But then again, neither am I now after this.
"How could I have lost the keys?"
I smack myself on the forehead.
Lost now within my head, my emotions,
I try to just pause and breathe, to calm,
      To stop beating myself up over it.
All eyes are on the ground as we walk back down the trail,
Five sets of eyes searching the ground:
Three children, the girls grouchy and tired;
The boy, still running wild though exhausted.
The parents are quiet,
      Both trying to keep their cool.
"How could you lose the car keys?"
"Where are they? Where could they be?"
"What are we going to do?"

Everyone keeps asking me, panic rising.

"I don't know!" I shout, shaking.

I'm lost within myself as I get,

        And everyone seems to take notice.

"We'll camp for one more night, I guess," my wife says.

She's trying her best to be calm

And doing much better at it than I.

"We'll keep looking," she continues.

"Someone should call about us if we're not back by tomorrow."

"We should camp close to the car then," I add.

"Flag a car down if we see one," I say,

        feeling defeated and quite the fool.

"Only if we can't find the keys,"

My wife says, trying to make me feel better.

I just simply smile and nod

        As we all continue looking.

The Fire Dancer

❖ ❖ ❖

I pulled a fire dancer from the flames.
He was too busy being drunk.
He didn't realize he was burning.
He was on fire, and I put it out.
And then we continued dancing,
Dancing and drinking around the fire,
Reveling in the cool night air.
I pulled a fire dancer from the flames.

I earned his respect, trust,
The fire dancer's love
Solidified in friendship, a bond.
Many nights we spent dancing around the flames,
Drunk within the fire's warmth,
And I became a healer.
He found comfort in my presence.

I pulled a fire dancer from the flames.
The alcohol had taken its toll on both of us,
But soon the fires became more infrequent.
The time of change had finally arrived.
Time to reenter the world with a newfound self.
We were changed by the fire.
Still I dance on.

Night Rains

❖ ◆ ❖

The night is moving in.
As the lightning strikes, it comes and goes,
The thunder cracking out both far and near.
A peaceful night's rest might be hard to find,
Leaving me with sporadic, brief moments to unwind.
Hearing the creatures of the night, I begin to fear,
For it's harder to tell who's friend or foe
Now in the dark night as the storm settles in.

As the clouds swirl around me,
The shadows dance back and forth
With the wind howling loud,
Blowing hard against my face.
I must seek shelter, a safe place,
Safe from the storm, far from the crowd,
For man will rob me of all I am worth,
Then lock me up for not paying my dues.

In Closing

Sitting with my back against a tree,
I slowly slouch myself all the way down
Until I am lying comfortably.

I rest my head back on the tree
As I breathe slowly—
Deep breaths in, deep breaths out.

Closing my eyes, I sink deeper in,
Becoming one with the earth and the tree
As the world around me shrinks.

I am calm, relaxed, whole.
I rest within the moment,
Gathering my energy to proceed.

I breathe calmly.
Then I rise, sitting back up,
Ready to begin anew.

4

Fragments of Thought

I

It's all right to cry; it doesn't make you any less,
For conquering yourself is one of life's greatest tests.
Weakness and strength, one in the same.
It's all about how you use them and the wisdom you gain.

❖ ❖ ❖

II

Why was zero jealous of eight? His belt.

❖ ❖ ❖

III

What do ya think? Man ... what do ya want to do?
It's snowin' and cold outside,
And I'm already tired of being cooped up.

We still have a long winter to go.
This is pretty much still just the start,
And I'm already feelin' these depressing winter blues.

❖ ❖ ❖

IV

I miss the party.
I miss the fun.
I miss a good time
And the taste of rum.

❖ ❖ ❖

V

Once again emptying out my stash,
The very last of my emergency cash,
All given to you
With never any return to me.
I don't know why I still do it,
Letting you take advantage of me.
That's not how I want things to be.
I just have trouble telling you no,
And it's probably why I can't let you go
    Either.

❖ ❖ ❖

VI

Unless you put your ear to the ground,
You will never hear the buffalo coming.
      Who then are the heathen gods you worship?
          Every year tonight,
I'm just trying to put pants on a monster.

VII

That stove gets hot when you turn it on,
      So be careful.

VIII

Just happy on the typewriter
Like a drugged-out housewife at her first job,
Life back in a simpler time,
But what do I actually know about that?

IX

Just trying to brainstorm
But worried about my flood of thoughts.
Will I be able to keep up?
Or will my barriers be overflown?
Causing me to lose hope in all that I've worked to build?
But I am positive and ready,
Barefoot, prepared to handle the flood.
Pen and paper in hand, I am ready to write.
I'm just trying to brainstorm,
To catch my thoughts like rain in a bottle
And put all these words down on paper.

❖ ❖ ❖

X

Well, I switched my brain to off,
And I never turned it back on.
It's been over a decade,
And I'm still chugging along.

❖ ❖ ❖

XI

Where did my creative spark go?
How can I regain my poetic flow?
To write beautifully once again
And be confident enough to let the world see.
To no longer hide my writings away
Like I always used to do,
And get out of my own way,
Something I'm not quite used to,
For I've always been quick to give up
And fast to get down on myself.

❖ ❖ ❖

XII

The morning mind is racing with ideas,
Running wild with options for the day,
To take care of the "have to do's"
And enjoy all the "want to do's,"
Hoping to feel good the entire way.

The evening mind is clouded and lost,
The thoughts of the day all repeating themselves
From all the things I did or didn't do,
Simply longing to experience something new.

❖ ❖ ❖

XIII

Gloomy, wet day.

Not much going on with it.

The lonely winter months are here,

Bringing with them seasonal depression.

Isolating myself inside to hide from the cold,

For I can't take my son out into the extremes.

He isn't ready to take on the element just yet,

So we are each other's only company.

He can't quite talk just yet,

But he's still my favorite person ever.

He is a light guiding me from darkness,

And I stay strong for him.

❖ ❖ ❖

XIV

I want to do some acid.

     I want to do some drugs.

I want to get drunk so very bad

     And smoke some big, fat, green nugs.

I want to get fucked up,

     Stumbling around, spilling my cup.

I want to be selfish

     And waste my life away,

But at this moment in time, I won't,

     But maybe again someday soon.

❖ ❖ ❖

XV

"You left your phone."

The text I send you.

Moments later your phone lights up in my hand.

"Oh …," I say.

Setting both phones down, I walk away

Since you are the only one I want to talk to.

❖ ❖ ❖

XVI

Straight-up honesty.

I miss being drunk and homeless,

But I can't live like that currently.

My son needs me to be able to take care of him

Because I am all he's got.

I'm his whole world right now,

His greatest protector,

And I cannot abandon him.

I will not,

For he is my whole world too,

My one and only child,

And I need him as much as he needs me.

I love him more than anything or anyone.

Some straight-up honesty.

❖ ❖ ❖

XVII

Chocolate milkshakes.
Living on borrowed time,
And I'm just grateful to still be alive.
Things could always be worse,
So I try to stay mindful of the present
Because I won't get this day back again.

❖ ❖ ❖

XVIII

I woke up in a good mood,
But that didn't last long.
You woke up with an attitude,
And suddenly my happiness was gone.

I just wanted some love,
But all we did was fight,
So I had to give myself a quick tug
To go back to feeling all right.

❖ ❖ ❖

XIX

Once I sat and watched the world go by.
Once I sat and waited for better things to come.
All that time I foolishly wasted,
All that time, my hurt-filled past.

It's time to let go of the hurtful past.

XX

Have you ever been down to the river to swim,
Losing yourself in the water and the fun,
And forgetting all your problems, at least for a little while?

XXI

I tried to put a shirt on,
     But I instantly got too hot.
Winter has now long since gone.
     Have wasted another shot.

XXII

If chocolate milk is being made,

    I would also like a glass,

        Please.

❖ ❖ ❖

XXIII

It's all right to cry, for it doesn't make you any less.

Conquering yourself is one of life's greatest tests.

Weakness and strength are actually one and the same.

It's all about how you use them and the wisdom you gain.

❖ ❖ ❖

XXIV

Some of them are folded, and some are just wadded up and thrown in.

I'm not sure what to do with them all.

Sad recycling days,

    Sad times for us all.

❖ ❖ ❖

XXV

Drunk on a longboard,
      Lying in the road.
Headlights approach, and I stagger up,
      Walking until the car goes past.
Nightlife living,
      Drunk and joyous,
Reveling in all the chaos,
      Some drunken, good-time anarchy.

❖ ❖❖ ❖

XXVI

I'm not stoned.
      I've just been meditating a lot lately.

❖ ❖❖ ❖

XXVII

He is the night, and he fears nothing.
We are the day and fear all things:
Dusk and dawn, our last connections.
And this is how we choose to spend them.
Oh, what truly foolish mortals are we!

❖ ❖ ❖

XXVIII

Free dinners, food I'm not responsible for,
Food cooked and prepared by those other than me,
A little something that costs me nothing.
Those are some meals I enjoy,
Yet I love to cook but simply not that often.
It's just a daily task, something I must do.
I'm simply cooking for survival.

❖ ❖ ❖

XXIX

Laughter from out of the darkness.
My son still lies awake back there,
In bed with Mom as she tries to wrestle him to sleep.

Grandma drinks Keystone, Papa drinks Pabst,
And they'll pass the joints around until you're flat on your ass.

❖❖❖

XXX

It is night, and the cool air flows,
The windows open and the fan blowing,
Letting in a fresh autumn breeze.
It's so peaceful; it's hard to believe
Happiness is an illusion,
A sick, twisted delusion.

❖❖❖

XXXI

Where has my mind gone,
All my creative thoughts,
My ability to put words on paper?
Lost out on some dude's lawn.
Now just a stain, a dirty spot.
Hustling and hoping for a caper,
Some quick, easy money—
That's what I want.
I don't want to have to struggle, honey.
So, no tricks now, you little cunt.
I don't want to fight.
I don't want no trouble,
Just peace in life,
And make that a double.

❖ ❖ ❖

XXXII

Pork taco dinner on a Friday night,
A cold November kind of night.
The coldness of winter is creeping in all around,
And the chaos of changing emotions begins to surround
Hostility and loneliness; anxieties abound.
I tire of living in constant fright.

XXXIII

Life is poetry.
You just have to know how to read it.
Simply look around you, and you're sure to see
That life is beautiful when it isn't ruined by man.
Do you not see the beauty of life all around you?
Because it is still there if you take a look.
All you have to do is open your eyes and see it.

XXXIV

Life is precious.
      You taught me that,
            The value of life.

❖ ❖ ❖

XXXV

I am bored with what's become regular.
I am so tired of the same daily routine.
I long for excitement; I want something new.

❖ ❖ ❖

XXXVI

When I think about talking with you,
I am myself; I express myself as so.
But when you are here, present with me,
My thoughts cloud, and I feel like a fool.

I try to practice what I want to say,
But then I fumble all my words when I speak.
Anxiety has my mind in a chokehold,
Making it so difficult for me to think clearly.

❖ ❖ ❖

XXXVII

I feel like my heart is empty of love
And all my patience has run out,
For I have grown tired of this domestic life,
Constantly trapped within my boredom and loneliness.

❖ ❖ ❖

XXXVIII

My spark has grown dim
          If it's not already died out,
And my patience has spread thin.
          I just want to scream, to shout.
Now with all my happiness gone,
I don't know how to say what's wrong.

❖ ❖ ❖

XXXIX

If the consequences are not carried out,
The rules will never be followed.
One's boundaries will always be overrun,
And peace of mind will never be maintained.
Happiness will always fall to depression,
A mediocre version of one's best reality.

❖ ❖ ❖

XL

Holding this razor blade
Ready, pressed up against my wrist,
My arms now more scars than skin.
Ready once again to feel that sweet metal kiss,
To harm myself, to cut and sin.

❖ ❖ ❖

XLI

I got shit to do.
    I got demands to meet.
        I got to stay functioning.

❖ ❖ ❖

XLII

I am tired,

Tired of simply existing

And not fully living.

But it's hard to live in this world.

The greed of man

Has changed all of society,

Everything revolving around money.

And if you have none,

You are left to struggle,

Making happiness harder to keep.

❖ ❖ ❖

XLIII

Go back to your church.

Go and read your "holy" Bible.

Go and leave me the fuck alone.

❖ ❖ ❖

XLIV

Thoughts of doom
Cloud my mind
As I sit alone.

Visions of death,
Frightening and realistic,
Cause me to begin to cry.

Haunted by these images,
My happiness now gone,
I fear for the future.

The cruel world of man
One day my son will enter.
How will the future be?

5

The Best Water I've Ever Had

There's an old man with a beard.

      He's wearing a long, gray cloak.

Seated upon a stump, he's smoking a pipe.

"Are you a wizard?" I ask as I draw nearer.

"Do I look like a wizard?" he replies.

"Kind of," I answer back.

"Well, let that be your opinion of it then," he states.

Hmm. How odd, I ponder.

He rises, supported by his walking staff.

"May I walk with you?" he asks.

      "It would be nice to have some company."

"Yes." I nod with a smile.

We continue walking down the trail.

"Forgive me for the slow pace," he says.

"It's all right," I respond.

      "It allows me to take in the view."

"Humph." He smirks. Smiling, he says,

      "I too enjoy the fresh mountain air."

We come upon a clearing up on a ridge,

      Where the trail splits off into two.

One follows along the ridgeline

      With an excellent view of the surrounding landscape.

The other leads up into a thick patch of trees.

It has the look more like an old game trail,

      As if carved out by the elk,

Their mighty antlers snapping off the dead branches
        As the herd passes through.
"Ah," says the old man,
        "Which path will you be taking?"
"I don't know yet," I answer.
"Well, might you decide in the morning?" he asks.
        "The sun will be setting soon.
And this looks like a very decent spot to camp,"
He adds after a moment of studying my face,
        Catching me lost in thought.
"That sounds like an excellent idea," I say.

And we each begin to set up our camps.
I hang my hammock up between two trees.
The spot has a very inviting feel to it,
As if it is welcoming me to sleep there,
        Like I am its honored guest.
The old man gathers wood to build a small fire.
When I finish setting up,
        I help by gathering more wood.
"Fancy dwellings," the old man jokes.
I drop my wood, piled by the fire.
"I like it," I say, smiling proudly,
        Maybe a tad defensive too.
"How are you going to sleep tonight?" I ask.
He looks at me for a moment.
Then he returns his gaze to the fire.
He takes a long drag from his pipe.
Exhaling, he simply nods.
"I sleep how I sleep."
        And that is all he says.

We sit high up on the mountain,
Watching the sun set over us
      And over the valley down below.
The night is calm and still.
The sky is clear, the stars beautiful.
We both sit before the fire, gazing up in silence.
Time seems to stop,
And the world around me feels nonexistent,
As if I have been swallowed up by the stars.

I catch myself yawning,
Coming back down into reality.
I notice my legs, butt; both are asleep and numb.
Stretching my arms up, I yawn again.
The old man notices and nods.
"I think it's time I retire for the night,"
      I say, standing up to go.
The old man nods again
As he continues to smoke his pipe.
"Have a good night," I say.
I make my way off toward my hammock.
"And you as well," he says as I go.
"Remember to think of which path you will take tomorrow,"
      I hear him say from within the night behind me.
Upon reaching my cozy, little hammock spot,
I ready myself for bed, for sleep, for rest.

I wake to the songs of the morning birds
As the sun just begins to rise.
It seems I slept peacefully all night,
      For I fell asleep as soon as I lay down.

I rise and start my morning routine,
Watching the sunrise as I go.
Then I notice the old man is gone,
Or he's at least nowhere I can see.
I continue with my morning,
Packing up all my gear.
Finished, I pull an apple out of my pack.

The fire is barely burning but still lit.
I breathe life back into it and feed it.
The morning is cool, the fire hot.
I enjoy its warmth while I eat my apple.
Leaves crunch, and a twig snaps behind me.
I turn to look, expecting to see the old man,
But a different figure emerges,
Coming up the trail the same as we have done.
As it approaches closer, I notice that it's a woman.

"Good morning," I say when she gets near.
"And good morning to you too,"
She responds with a smile.
"May I rest here by your fire with you for a moment?" she asks.
Looking up at her, I notice her beauty.
She catches me staring, and I look away.
"You're welcome to it," I say,
My cheeks blushing red.
She sits down in the spot where the old man sat the night before.
Reaching into her pack, she removes a jug of water.
She takes a drink and catches me staring again.
"Sorry," I say to her, blushing again.
But she just smiles and laughs

While taking another big swig of her jug.

    She then offers me a drink.

"It's just water," she says,

    Wiping her mouth off with her sleeve.

I accept it and take a drink.

"This is really good water, nice, clean, and ice cold,"

    I say after taking another, deeper swig.

"Where did you happen to come across this?" I ask.

She looks at me and then laughs a moment.

"It's from a small stream north of my village," she answers.

"I filled all of my containers with it before starting my adventure,

And I only have a little left."

Handing her jug back, I say, "Thanks."

The sun has now near fully risen,

    Leaving the sky a beautiful morning blue.

As the air begins to radiate warmth,

She pulls her hood down and shakes her hair loose.

I watch as she does this,

Staring again, amazed by her beauty.

But her actions reveal what her hood was hiding.

    She has pointed ears.

"You're an elf!" I say, taken aback, shocked.

She tenses, frozen with panic.

"I've never met an elf before," I say more calmly.

Her panic starts to ease.

"Or perhaps you have just never noticed,"

    She proclaims, looking calm once more.

"You're right," I say. "I'm sorry. I wasn't trying to offend.

    I just didn't notice until I saw …"

"Until you saw my ears," she interrupts.

"If you have a problem with elves, I will leave,"

      She says after a moment of silence.

"No, no, you are more than welcome to stay,"

      I tell her reassuringly.

She looks at me and starts to smile.

"It is rare for me to have company on my travels," I say,

"But yesterday I was joined by an old man and today you."

"What happened to the old man?" she asks.

"I don't know," I answer.

"I have not seen him yet this morning."

We are both silent for a moment.

"I must confess," she begins.

"I saw your fire from my camp last night.

And I rushed up the trail this morning," she continues.

"I was hoping to catch up with you before you started for the day."

I look at her, slightly puzzled, but then she continues speaking.

"I fear I am being followed, and there is safety in numbers.

      I hope to find someone trustworthy to travel with."

"Well, you are most welcome to travel with me," I say,

"And you can decide for yourself about my trustworthiness."

She laughs as I joke.

"What do you know of the trails ahead?" I ask. "Of the split?"

Glancing over to where the trail forks,

We both stare for a long moment.

"I think the old man knew something,

But he didn't share it with me,"

I say, finally breaking the silence.

"The path that goes up looks mostly like a game trail,"

She responds, "but neither seems to be much traveled."

I nod, agreeing, and add,

"This is not a common area for people to wander.

I feel like the ridgeline path is the right way to go

Unless this upper way is some new shortcut."

"Bandits are known for making false trails to confuse

And rob unsuspecting travelers," she states matter-of-factly.

"Do you have much experience dealing with bandits?" I inquire.

She turns, looking away; she avoids the question.

"Well, I don't know where the old man went,

So, shall we start walking without him?" I ask.

She gives me an approving nod.

The two of us rise and start to ready ourselves.

She starts walking to the fork in the trail,

While I make sure the fire is put out.

       Then I hurry to catch up with her.

She's stopped at where the trail forks,

Waiting for me, studying tracks along the paths.

"It seems your companion has gone on ahead of us,"

       She says when I catch up to her.

Strange of him not to wait, I think.

So, we start off down the ridgeline path,

The same way he went sometime earlier.

The walk is quiet, neither of us speaking much.

I am lost in my thoughts.

Why did the old man leave without me?

What time did he leave to get such a head start?

Did he know about the elvish girl following us?

Suddenly, my thoughts are interrupted.

She has stopped walking, stooping down.

       She studies the ground intently.

"His tracks have stopped,"
She whispers under her breath,
     Slightly alarmed.
She has become very still, intense,
Listening to trees around us.
I think it is quite odd behavior,
But I don't pay it that much mind.
She studies the surrounding area for quite some time.
"His tracks have vanished. Let's keep moving," she says fearfully.
And we both start walking again.

We hike until the heat of the day
Drives us to take refuge in some shade.
Resting among a group of trees,
She pulls out her container of water.
After taking several long drinks,
She offers some to me.
"I don't want to drink up all the last of your good water," I say.
"It's all right. It's good to share," she persists.
And I've got to say that I'm glad she shared,
Because that water was some of the best I have ever had.

Notes

In the poem "Channeling the Moon Doggie," (page 66) lines *1 and *2 are separate quotes from the movie *The Beach Bum*.

Korine, Harmony, director. *The Beach Bum* [Film]. Iconoclast Films, 2019. 1 hr., 36 min.

Index of Titles and First Lines

Printed in the United States
by Baker & Taylor Publisher Services